OPENING THE SHUTTERS
Poems
by
Nan Knighton

© 2022 Nan Knighton

MOTHER AT 73 and I KNOW HOW TO DO THIS! previously published in *The Michigan Quarterly Review*

2022 Knight Errant Music

ISBN 978-1-66782-115-3
eBook ISBN 978-1-66782-116-0

www.nanknighton.com

Praise for OPENING THE SHUTTERS

"*Opening the Shutters* is a glorious book, and Nan Knighton is a remarkable writer. This set of poems feels like going on a holiday with your best friend: a daughter, a wife, and a mother who has thought deeply about what it means to live out each of these stages of life just a little more deeply than the rest of us. The poems in this collection are specific and tactile, each one a small story of a moment worth living. Taken together, they paint an entire lifetime of thoughtful joy. They are earned happiness for all of us who are tried in the furnace but emerge the better for it. I urge anyone who loves poetry not to miss this book."

Ken Ludwig, author of Tony and Olivier Award Winners *Lend Me a Tenor* and *Crazy for You*

"Reading Nan Knighton is like reading a 21st century Edna Millay. Her poems are quick, deft, unpretentious, and they're full of surprises. Surprise, in fact, is one of her main themes – the surprises of love (both its beginning and its end), of those moments when, out of the blue, happiness comes upon you unbidden. She can even make poetry out of the shock of finding pigeons in her bathroom."

Charles McGrath, Former Editor of *The New York Times Book Review*

"Extraordinary, enchanting and so alive, Nan Knighton's poems have imagined a magical journey into worlds we wished we lived in, and believe we have. *Opening the Shutters* is a remarkable book."

Delia Ephron, author of *Siracusa* and a screenwriter of *You've Got Mail*

"I know Nan Knighton's glorious work from the theatre. And now I have fallen in love with her poetry. Her newest book *Opening the Shutters* is a wonderful collection of poems blending the rhythms of human life and observations in such a lyrical and visual way. I read it in one sitting. Stunning!"

Richard Ridge, *Broadway World*

"Nan Knighton's poems celebrate the ebb and flow of everyday life. They capture with carefully chosen clarity what it feels like to be alive in the first quarter of the twenty first century."

Alfred Uhry, Pulitzer Prize winner for
Driving Miss Daisy

"As the title *Opening the Shutters* implies, Nan Knighton's new collection of poetry startles in its buoyant embrace of sensations, fully inhaled like fresh air. Her poems fly. They take risks...with arresting images, kick-ass verbs, hilarious dialogue and dramatic power. Such a distinctive and original voice. I had to keep reading. Brilliant."

Elizabeth Goodenough
Secret Spaces of Childhood

Praise for THE SCARLET PIMPERNEL

"With book and lyrics by Nan Knighton and a musical score by Frank Wildhorn, the Tony Award-nominated musical is a little bit pop, a little bit camp and a lot of fun... Delightful."

Pam Kragen, *San Diego Tribune*

"A light-hearted, prettily appointed entertainment...a show that moves with speed...and is never solemn for very long."

Vincent Canby, *New York Times*

"This swashbuckling musical comedy features soaring melodies by composer Frank Wildhorn (*Jekyll & Hyde*) and a witty book and delightfully droll lyrics by Nan Knighton (*Saturday Night Fever*)."

Robert W. McDowell, *Classical Voice of North Carolina*

Praise for SATURDAY NIGHT FEVER

"Nan Knighton's book...understand(s) the desire to get out of your own skin that brings people to the discos over and over."

Richard Sanford, *Columbus Underground*

Praise for CAMILLE CLAUDEL

"This book, written by Nan Knighton [book and lyrics] with music by Frank Wildhorn, reveals a magnificent love story. [It] has the momentum of a huge wave. By the end it crashes down on the shore with a tremendous thunder that shakes you."

Paroles D'Artiste

For John, Eliza and Nola

CONTENTS

PART 4: HOME

PART 5: MOM & DAD

PART 6: THE GROWN-UP

I STILL HEAR THE BELLS
(A Note on Poetry)

Some people just don't like poetry. Sometimes I don't like poetry. There's an impatience which can set in right off the bat. Novels give us a plot line. We follow the characters. We know where we are. With poems, we're asked to step into limbo. So why go there? For me, it's because I like the mystery. I like surprise and the quick hit of a poem. Poems can ambush us in one page, one line even. They may incite us or serenade us, make us laugh or draw us into feelings which reflect our own, and a poem can, quite suddenly, transform what we see. It's as if we're in the same room as the poet who has handed us a kaleidoscope.

But a poem can be much more than that. In May of 2021, I read that in Myanmar, 40 poets had been jailed. 4 others were shot in the head, bodies incised from neck to belly and then burnt. So what's this horror all about? Why kill *poets*? Why are *poets* considered so dangerous? Is it because they can't be broken? In prison, without pen and paper, they continue to write poems, memorizing their own words or using rocks to carve them into stone walls. A few of these poems have emerged, God knows how – even more evidence of the insistence of these poets upon reaching out, being heard. I read one of these poems. It was quite short, possibly passed on by word of mouth only. It's the very last line that stays with me, a line which tells us all we need to know about the irrepressible spirit of the poet. The line reads:

I still hear the bells and all is well.

OPENING THE SHUTTERS
Poems
by
Nan Knighton

PART 1
NEW YORK

RELEASED!

The moon is rising! We've come to a party at
The Water Club and no one can resist staring
out the windows at the East River rushing by,
a stretch of silver in the dark

and look at all these lawyers! It's a party for
lawyers. They've been released into the
night, boozing, buzzing, gibing, slapping
backs and there's a hunger in the air

and a gleaming dance floor with a band whose
trumpeter is leaning clean out of his body.
Couples dance, couples laugh. We are all
just letting chicken go cold on our plates

and I feel so *young.* I'm drinking crisp clear wine
and I'm ravished anew every time I turn and
stare at that silver river surging, rushing and
one jaunty lawyer reaches for me and says

"Dance with me, baby!" And he swoops me
off my feet and says I'm light as air, and we
laugh and do a tango which I have no idea how
to do! For a moment I forget about my children.

Suddenly we see it. We're all pointing out the
windows and laughing. There, on the water,
a yacht is sailing by – an immense white yacht is
sliding through the river like Cleopatra's barge

and now we see through the windows of the yacht
people *dancing*, and they're all dressed in white,

men and women dancing, hoisting glasses of
champagne. And they *wave* to us and we start
waving back, still laughing at this sudden
splurge of romance. And I feel *free!* I am on the
water! I am shaking back my curls, kicking off my
shoes, whirling in the hot, steamy air

and the river rushes, rushes, carries off the
glittered yacht toward the moon. We dance! The
trumpeter is 16 again and blaring, flaunting!
No one knows what time it is.

A TOUCH OF GRANDEUR

"Brrrrp." I raise my head.
"Brrrrp, Brrrrp."
"Uh-oh," I say.
"What *now?*" he whines,
my sleeping husband. "It's 6:00 A.M.!"
I say, "Pigeons in the bathroom."
"Don't be ridiculous," he snarls. "You're dreaming."
"Brrrrp, Brrrrp, Brrrrp…" (*Pause*)
He hauls himself from the bed in
his new navy blue Calvin Klein briefs,
goes to stand in the bathroom doorway.
"Well," he says, "there are pigeons in the bathroom."

I scurry over. Yep. Not dreaming.
One pigeon perches on the sink. The other
struts back and forth between the Listerine
and the Neutrogena Body Oil. "*Shit*," he says.
"You left the bathroom window open all last
night!" (*Pause*) "Go get a broom."
I run for the broom, a banshee with my tangled
morning hair, tear back, heart whomping.
Armed with the broom, he ventures – one step-
onto the tiled floor, then a JAB to the air and-
WHOOSH! The pigeons fly! Feathers Flail!
He *bolts* back, knocks me over, my head
whacking into wall, diamonds showering
through my eyes.

The pigeons simply settle back down, eyeing us
with distaste. He stands thoughtful with his broom.
"We'll close the door," he says. "Eventually they'll

fly back out." We close the door. Now he's in a state
because he can't get at his hair gel – *"Shit!"* He flings
out the door for work, even more displeased than
the pigeons, who do finally wing off. But all day
I feel a touch of grandeur. Somewhere…brrrrping
in Manhattan…are birds of my personal acquaintance.

ON A SUMMER AFTERNOON

I am sitting here naked in the heat.
I am writing songs.
Caught in a heaviness of thought,
I look up through my window.
Across the alley in that building
just past the garage, I see a man.
He is standing at his window,
tending a limp geranium.
He is middle-aged, thick-bellied,
deep into the business with his plant.
He is completely nude.

Here we are on a summer afternoon,
he and I, nurturing things,
I in my building, he in his,
both our bodies a bit worse for wear.
We are bare, at ease with our aging,
and there are thousands of us,
at this moment, at our windows,
drifting in our heads, breathing in
this oversoft air, quite mortal.
How quiet it is.
I go back to work.

PEOPLE LIVE HERE

When I was a child, my father drove us
once a year to New York for a weekend
at The Pierre, where we walked along
emerald green carpeting, stepped into
hushed elevators whose operators
whisked us up to our rooms, then down
again for lunch at the Pierre Grill where
Indians in turbans served curry from
a cart. There was Room Service for my
brother and me: a bowl of pretzels, two
cokes and our own bucket of ice!
Glamorous pigeons warbled on the
windowsills. Restaurants beckoned with
rolls and cold sweet butter. And after
dinner, we'd ride a Checker Cab down
to the harbor where we gazed upon
glimmering ocean liners. Oh, New York,
New York – it was my destiny! But (and this
was a fairly big "but") the fact that people
lived here had me spooked.

I mean, my God, what sort of people lived
here? Movie stars – yes, sure. Gangsters,
sure. But families? In this explosive city?
I couldn't envision it – a mom type person
in the kitchen: "Kids, Granny's coming over!
Let's all make fudge!" Kids: "Okay! Yay!"
Also, it was clear to me that any kid who
had recess on top of a roof would end up
unhinged. Oh, and by the way, how could
anybody sleep in this town? I never did.

As a child, I lay awake in hotel sheets,
mesmerized by honking.

My conclusion at that point in time: Anyone
who chose of their own free will to LIVE
in New York City was... spooky.

Basically, that's what I still think, and here's
my theory: it's the elevators. We spend so
much time in these wooden boxes, stepping
through sliding doors, pushing buttons,
going down and up, up and down, landing
with a thunk, flying out lobby doors and then
there's an interlude (the day) before heaving
back into the elevators with our worried dogs
and banging shopping bags. Let's face it.
Elevators have us right where they want us.

So, yes, I have to say that most of us
New Yorkers are a little off – not exactly
misfits, but spooky enough that we don't
seem to really fit in anyplace else, unless
it was like – no, I can't think of anyplace else.
We're just people who live here. I do however
want to note that I'm sure right now somewhere
in this city, someone is making fudge.

I KNOW HOW TO DO THIS!

At 2:00 a.m. I unlatch the giant window,
this porthole which gapes out across the
reservoir. *Whap!* Moist wind belts my face!
Below me, the trees along Fifth Avenue
are great fans of yellow, rained upon and
drying now like blousy laundry. Lamplight
and cloudlight ride the air. I lean out.
The wind comes stronger. No one would
understand if I went tumbling out my
porthole. They'd just find me on the sidewalk,
a gnarl of squashed pajamas. And anyway,
tonight I don't want to die.

Tonight I want to fly! I *know* I've flown before.
My arms stretch into the air. My body
is straining at the bit. I know how to do this!
I swear, right now I could streak out across
those drowsy trees, nose-dive the reservoir,
and then, like the gulls, simply dip my toes
into that warm black water – Up again! Lunge,
blitz the sky! Oh to just let out one whoop-
Halloo! To holler, hoot into the wind –
Hello, halloo! And maybe I wouldn't fall.
Maybe I wouldn't die. Maybe I'd just be
this joyous fling, these flying pajamas!

THE BAT JOB

August 3rd. 11:00 p.m. John shouts,
"There's a bird in the living room." Wow.
Nola and I come running. There's a
small winged creature zipping figure-8s
in the air. "Honey," I say to my husband,
"That's not a bird. That's a bat."

I get on the phone. (I am really very good
in a crisis.) No one's home at the A.S.P.C.A.
I call 311. I say, "We've got a bat."
The 311 Lady and I talk it over. "Listen,"
she says, "you've got to get rid of that bat.
I'm connecting you to the police."
And she does. The Police Lady says,
"We're sending a squad car."

Ding-Dong.
Two cops, guns strapped to their sides,
saunter into the living room and we all see
absolutely nothing. The very tall cop asks,
"Is this for real?"
I say, "I have heard that bats like curtains."
(I do know my animals.)
They all ignore me till we spot the bat
clinging to the curtains.

The redheaded cop radios in. He says,
"We're here on the bat job." He asks for
reinforcements – a third cop who has
special gloves. Nola says, "Would you guys
like some coffee?" They say yes, quite pleased.

Ding-Dong.

The third cop arrives, beaming ear-to-ear.

He says, "I came all the way from Paris for this job."

I ask if they've ever caught a bat before.

"Nope," says the very tall cop. "Had a

boa constrictor once – yeah, you could hear

it in the next room, knocking over

chairs." Nola brings coffee for all.

The problem now is that the cop with the

special gloves forgot to bring the gloves.

"Okay," says the very tall cop, "everyone stand back."

He grabs today's *New York Times*, whaps into the curtains

and the bat falls to the floor. Thud. We gasp.

The cop who came from Paris sips his coffee, then says,

"Got a box?"

Gingerly, with a handkerchief, the bat is dropped

into a shoebox. The redheaded cop radios in again.

"Yeah," he says, "it's the bat job. The bat is D.O.A.

We're deciding what to do with the corpse."

When they leave, the shoebox tucked beneath his arm,

the very tall cop says, "Well, I want to thank you folks.

This was the most fun I've had since the boa constrictor."

Everybody wants to hug.

Instead we high-five. Many times. Some fist-bumps.

We have all fallen in love.

We know the bat job will live on and

reading the *New York Times* again

will be a bit problematic.

COFFEE SHOP WRITER

August Wilson went to bars to write. I go to
coffee shops. I'm a mother. Mothers do not
leave their families at night to go to bars.

And so I sit here at the counter with the hum
of 4:00 P.M. There's an old gentleman two seats
down from me. He has hot coffee and a Danish
and the waitress asks him, "How's the Danish?"
He says, "I like it a lot." He says it gently, as if
he were reviewing Proust. He reminds me of my
father, and for one moment I'm afraid I might cry.

A waiter with ruddy cheeks wipes down the counter.
The old gentleman asks him if he has children and
the waiter says, "Yeah, there's little Barney, who's 2,
and little Jimmy, who's 7, and Jack, who's 11."
The old man says, "God bless" and smiles. Sitting
here with these people, I miss Baltimore. I think of my
parents, 78 and 81, with two new kittens careening
around their apartment. Two weeks ago, when I went
home to visit, Mother bought all my favorites – petit-fours
for dessert, scrapple for breakfast – as if I were 19 again
and only home from college for the weekend, and I
lay on the floor by the fire, playing with the kittens
and I didn't want to leave.

The old gentleman has finished his Danish now.
Does he know he's become my father? He is in
no hurry to leave here. Neither am I. I do feel 19
again, sitting here in my jeans and old flannel shirt.
I wonder what would I do differently, were I to start

over. Would I never marry, live alone with some cats and dogs and write night and day? Oh, I *would* make life simpler. How could I have known in my 20's the warmth of simplicity, the open sky of solitude?

The waitress asks the old gentleman if he wants more hot coffee. "No," he says, pleasantly.
"It's just dandy right now."

Yes, it's just dandy right now.

NIGHTS AT MARLOWE'S

I think it's a Brazilian restaurant now.

Back then it was Marlowe's
(and this was in the days when
people smoked and kissed in
bars and voices grew too loud)
and there we'd go, James and I and
David, woven raw through each other,
gouging for secrets, gripping a wrist
or a thigh, to make a *point* within
that waterfall of confusion which
smelled of winter, whiskey, Marlboros.
"I love you, I *love* you," we'd snarl and
slam our fists on the bar. Sometimes
James would cry. We overlapped,
stung with epiphanies, and they
wouldn't kick us out till 1:00 or 2:00,
when only actors wandered 46th Street,
so late I could catch a cab in a snap.

One dark and blowy night, drifting
home in a cab, drunk, tears falling,
wind spilling cross my face, I prayed.
I don't know what I prayed.
I just remember someone listening-
right outside the window as we whipped along-
someone smiling, listening to my prayer.
I know I said "Thank you." I know that
angels find their way into bars and watch
as friends slam fists and touch too much.
I know I said, "Thank you."

WIFE IN DRAG

They are passing round the Chevre Pizzettes,
Moroccan Shrimp, Yellow Fin Tuna on Taro
Chips. Red and pink tulips sprout like trees from
each marbled table top. The host blusters by,
a diamond pin twinking his lapel. My husband is
regaling old gals who gleam and clink in golden
chains and chokers. My husband pulls aside
slick-haired men to whisper, "We should talk…"
My husband is the plumed, dancing bird.

I am the body in the yellow silk dress with its
feet in the black patten heels. I'm the wife in drag,
keeling through this parlor where seasoned
smiles pop like ping-pong balls. I come to a
window and look down. On the sidewalk below,
three sweaty kids jump rope as twilight sprawls
around them. They've got no use for tomorrow.

I lean on the windowsill. If they look up,
they'll see a soldier in her army jacket.
They'll hoot, "Come on down!"

"Those children should be supervised,"
says a voice at my shoulder. I turn to see
an empress, sprinkled with sapphires.
I say, "Oh well, they're just playing."
She smiles, says, "And who are you?"
And I can't answer.

SUNDAY EVENING ON THE
VERRAZANO NARROWS

She's a lifter of clouds, swooping
across the cold March sky.
With a sigh, she breathes in
this last keel of lavender light.

I've never seen a bridge before
so unassuming in its beauty.
She seems to have simply
risen from the sea one day,
whispered up by the fish.

I can hear her wires strumming,
humming, drawing me in, a hymn,
a prayer, and now, as night folds
about her, slowly, half in love,
I see her stretch her silver limbs
to welcome in, like children,
this band of blurry stars.

I HEAR THEM SINGING

I want to know what happened.
I need to know where they are.

We called them "Bag Ladies." Do you remember? Swathed
in black, they'd heave through the afternoon shadows with
crumpled shopping bags and sharp shifting eyes. And you'll
remember, I'm sure, how they muttered to their phantoms, and
how all the clean people would weave away from the mutters
and the soot, the rags and bottles spilling from their bags.
And then one day, the clean people noticed that, well, they just
seemed to…disappear. But where did they go? I need to know.

Are you too young to recall? Try to picture them as night fell,
sinking down onto the stoops, splaying wide their bursting
legs, slumping back against stone walls for the hours of
jabbering air and, like great whooshing whales, crooning to
each other of the lives they'd never lived – *Once I drank from
silver cups… Rubies flounced about my neck… I rode
high-stepping horses…* All those voices echoing through the
dark, dark fragments of the night

But can you tell me where they are now? It's important, you see,
because one day as I was crossing the street – *suddenly* – there
she stood, a woman swathed in black. She smiled at me, her
eyes sharp and shifting. She whispered, "Why do you keep your
distance?" And I ran. But it's pointless, you'll agree, to run when
you know you've been found out.

I need you not to fear. Let's not fear, you and I. There is no way
to deafen them as they sing uneasy songs, knowing they will never
find their way out of tonight. And they know I am mere steps from

the jabber and the mutter. And they wait for me to come. You understand? I'm meant to sit with them on the cold winter stoops, chanting and pretending there is never any pain.

I don't know where they are. But I hear them singing.

PART 2
ELSEWHERE

ON THE FERRY

We are on the ferry, my two daughters and I.
One daughter is almost eight, freckled
and fresh. The other, a five-month-old doll,
flops in my arms. Suddenly! the fog horn blows:
a dragon bellowing into the sky!
The baby jerks, looks up – she stares at Death
head-on for the first time. She screams.
I have her clutched to my breast.
"Mommy's here, Mommy's here…" She gapes
at me in terror: why don't I make it go away?
Again, huge and mean, it roars through the fog.

My other daughter turns from the window,
a quiver at her lips. "I want to cry, too,"
she says. "Then do," I say. She comes to
my other arm and I hold her. Her hair
smells of strawberry shampoo, and a tear
eases into each blue eye.

The fog horn booms! My baby screams!
The older girl presses her head into me.
I keep them warm in my arms,
these two, sprung out of me, seven years
apart, these two children who are mine.
And the older one says, "I'm angry.
My sister is scared. That makes me angry."
I hold them both, saying,
"Mommy's here, Mommy's here…"
And as we steer slowly into sun again,
the older pops her head up and smiles at me.

"Mommy, you were crying, too?
Why were you crying?"
The baby sleeps.

AT THE SEAWALL: PALM BEACH

Tonight there's a yellow moon. Buttery light
mottles the black sea. My husband and I
sit here on a wooden bench at the seawall.
We stretch our feet on the pedicured grass
and stare out to sea. We are 35 and 36
and wonder why we're here.

A bronze Rolls Royce oozes along the road
behind us. It pauses, motor thrumming, as
two white-haired gentlemen gaze outward
at the sea. A Maurice Chevalier moment.
The Rolls purrs away, swallowed in these
palmed avenues of banks, banks, more
banks. Hey, look – it's another bank!

Today in the pharmacy, we stumbled on a huge
rack of wooden canes, canes, more canes.
We nudged each other, we were 17 again, and
fled out the door, laughing, "Shhh!," laughing.

Now three ladies, blown brittle by the night
breeze, approach the seawall, arm in arm in arm,
all their arms bedazzled with wrinkles. They
sniff the air, eyes veering toward the sea.
One of them whispers, "Listen to that…"
All of us listen. What are we listening to?
The moon bubbling in the waves? The lady
whose smile never leaves her face, turns
to us. "Oh, my dears," she says, "I hope you
will come back one day and hear what you
cannot hear now." But we *do* hear, hour

after hour through the night, that lilt in her voice which beckons and beckons us into her world. Too soon, too soon!

AND THERE WERE GIANTS
(...in Sarasota, long ago...)

When I was five, Florida was savage.
I wore a Seminole headdress and quivered
at the blood red faces splotched onto
coconuts. Parrots challenged my eye, their
feathers a furor of colors. Leering crocodiles
perched in cement pits, never ever moving
as they whispered to me of treachery.
I rode in a glass-bottom boat where yellow
fish slid underneath, lit by some undersea sun.
And the Flamingo Gardens! These impossibly
tall creatures mincing by, spitzing and lifting
spindly legs and do I only imagine that suddenly
they rose as one and flew into the fluttering sky?

And there were giants. Yes, truly – giants, retired
from the circus, who came to Florida to live.
Mother read about them – two giants ran the
Seawinds Motel on Route 1. A husband and a wife.
Daddy promised we'd drive by. Maybe we'd see a
giant crossing a courtyard, shaking out the laundry,
cannonballing into a pool, their splashes exploding
the sky. And so we drove. I looked right, left, right
for the Seawinds Motel, throat tight, heart sparking.
Then came the cry:

"There she is!"
My head whipped to the left. "*Who?!*"
"The giant's wife! There was a wall and–"
"*Where?!*"
"We saw her head above a wall. She was

walking by behind a stone wall!"

I cannot explain how it haunts me still. For one
racing moment, I'd looked away. And in that
moment, I'd missed my giant's head, her hair
a swarm of tangles, her eyes defiant of intruders.

And years go by, years of returning to Florida,
always hoping to retrieve my savage land
of clamping crocodile jaws and skies that swim
with frantic pink birds. And always I am in search
of the whopping heads of giants, gliding over
stone walls, their eyes hot and haughty. These
are the faces of my Florida – barbarous, bedazzling,
imbued with the vehemence of memory.

HERE AT THE CASA MARINA

Joint's jumpin' tonight. At least down here it is. I'm on
this wooden deck with my rum and cigarettes. Inside
the hotel, they're unsullied. Reputations are upheld.
Here in the open air, we happily go to hell. The waiters
wear shorts and scurry. The laughing's raw and quick.
The air smells of crisp beer and floaty smoke. It's
midnight. Somewhere inside my husband and my
children sleep, drugged with sun. But I need to be
out here, where I'm 19, more boy than girl, thin and
revved. The waiters simply note: here's that woman
again, the one who comes at night to write.
They don't know I'm a rogue.

My children insist that I be their mother, craving a
soft-voiced lady, drifting flowers down into a vase.
My husband wraps me in at night, too tight, insisting I be
nothing but his warm wife person. He hates the roar
inside my head that pulls me out here. Well, I don't ask
for understanding. That's a big thing. I ask only for these
hours here, *anywhere*. Light the match! The cage blasts
open and I scramble from my skin and *no one* belts me back.

I am galloping across the sand, swinging my sword.
I am sweat and sex and beating wings.
Let me be!

WHY NOT?

I am standing on this skimpy beach.
There are no pompous beaches in Key West,
and no one's here right now but me and
these two mutts who gallop down the pier.
Sun simmers, falls, lapsing into water.
Waves flick and nuzzle at the rocks.
Someone has airbrushed this high, high sky
plush pink. One cloud heaves a sigh.

Beauty here is halfbreed, unrehearsed,
like these two dogs who now hit the sand.
They are tropical mutts with no clear owner.
The small tawny male pursues the great
white lady. He's desperate to have her.
She's gracefully indifferent.
She could have him for breakfast.

Way, way out, boats slip across the sea,
misted, illusory, while here the dogs
are hurling through the palm trees.
She laughs, ramming him off.
He's panting, so hard at work,
swerving through the swelling shadows.
I'd really like to console him.

And then she simply stops. Her eyes rest on
the dark sea. The goddess gives it up, holding
still as her suitor stretches up his full height
and mounts one glorious white leg.
He pumps at that leg, august, ennobled.
I suppose she just decided: Oh, why not?
Really. Given the blur of life, why not?

LEAVING KEY WEST: 1989

People here applaud the setting of the sun.
Crowding together on the pier,
drinks in hand, they watch as the sun
drops into the water, melting like a jewel.
The mystery is not that they applaud,
but that nowhere else in the world
do people think to do this.

I stand now in the dark, watching as
the moon eases out from the clouds,
sniffing sky. I know tomorrow I must
leave here and am still only on the edge
of understanding this island where
the palm trees reign. And I sigh,
I succumb, as they dip downward,
rustling the air, or as they slap and rattle
their fronds in an afternoon rain. By night
they acquiesce to brash hotel lights
splashing up their spines, for after all,
they do not object to being showy.
So – goodbye, you beauties.

And goodbye to rose-flushed skies,
snooty pelicans and afternoon light that
skims the sea like tossed glitter. Goodbye
to the rough sands dotted with broken shells
and swirls of fresh tar. Goodbye to fat,
wandering cats and goodbye to the
roosters and chickens, those strutting
bums who insist they own the streets.

Goodbye to this extravagantly humid air.
Goodbye to jazz bands, greasy diners and
pleasantly crumbling people. Goodbye to all
the sloppy, bow-legged dogs and farewell
to the one steadfast dog who sat on a deck,
head held high. Seems to me it would be
a pretty good life to be a boat dog.

Impossible to understand this island, but I know
we reach a point where our souls start clamoring
to be set loose again. So I come here. Here we
give in to rustling palms and suns that melt like
jewels into the sea. Here we find a new world.

VERNA

Up on a horse again.
Swing the right leg over. Creak
of the saddle, tang of the leather,
hand on the horn and I'm home.

These trails reel with dust,
sink for the thud of worn hooves.
Three dozy wranglers cruise alongside,
looping lassos over scrub brush,
gibing, razzing at each other.
Cattle peer up from the valley.

My horse Verna walks smack
into a bush, six feet high. She
sways so it scratches at her belly.
I am laughing, battling briars.
One wrangler sings back at me,
"Yep, that's Verna, all right."

Verna clean sails me cross a gulley.
My heart gets so full, I stand in the
stirrups, see the hills hot and gold.
Verna stops to heave one huge leg
back, kicking at the flies. I am
wildly happy.

TO THE BLOND GUY IN AUSTRALIA

We are petting kangaroos. I barely breathe,
crouching on the ground, stroking the fur of a
joey. The mother simply eyes me. Ver-y care-fully.
Emus stalk about like traffic cops gone nuts.
You can do this? You can just walk around here
stroking and dodging wild animals? Like a snap
of the fingers, one kangaroo lands a ten foot
bound beneath these odd and bending trees.
I am laughing, whispering, "Wow..."

Two young fathers come to sit with us, their
children at their sides. They explain, "Saturdays
we get the kids. The girls get their hair done."
The kids and I run our hands down the baby
kangaroo. We tell them we've come from
New York. The blond guy smokes, nods.
"Yeah, I went to Madrid once – this town in Spain."
The air is sweet. The emus toss and squawk.

The guys pull cans of beer from a bag, take a few
swills and offer some to us. When we say no, but
thanks, the blond one looks down. He says, "Guess
you think of us over here just drunk all the time."
"*No*," I say. "I've *never* thought that." I watch as his
child comes near to place a hand on his father's neck.

We get up to leave. I'll never see the soft-eyed blond
again. Never. Nor probably Australia, where life's
as easy as Summer, 1950. I ask this man if he might
someday come to New York, but he shrugs and sips
his beer. "No. When I went to that Madrid, I just wanted

to come home." After a moment, he smiles.

We drive back to Sydney. I can hardly speak.
My hands still smell of kangaroo.

RETURNING TO REHOBOTH BEACH

Augusts in Rehoboth. We were 14, 15, 16, my
friends and I, and every night some primal force
thrust us back onto the boardwalk with its smells of
sun-trodden wood, creosote drifting up and melding
with the lush smell of popcorn, buttery popcorn,
caramel popcorn, sweet whiffs floating from
Dolles salt water taffy, the hot, crusty aroma spilling
out of Grotto pizza and the ocean – *right there* – you
could hear the waves, soft, undulant. And there was
Zoltar – grim and exotic, spitting out his fortunes.
And Skee-Ball – the roll of the balls, the clunk when
they landed – I always figured that could count as
the one (and only) sport in which I excelled! God,
Rehoboth – it made my heart beat fast just to
remember. "Let's go for my birthday," I said to
my husband. He said, "*Really?*" But he could see
the wanderlust in my eyes.

So yesterday we checked into the grand Henlopen
Hotel, which has seen better days, but it *is* still here.
Straight to the boardwalk – Oh, I'd forgotten the photo
booths! And yes, there were the dreaded bumper cars
where kids still jolted by with savage smiles. Night fell
and still in the shadows teenagers angled for mystery.
The ocean mirrored the yellow moon, such a swoony
moon splashing light onto the dune grass. And suddenly
we knew it was time for Fried Dough.

So we sat on a weathered wooden bench to wolf it down
and it was just about then that we noticed we were the
oldest people on the boardwalk. Huh.

We made a study of it, scrutinizing everyone who walked by-
fat people, grey-haired people, one man in a motorized
wheelchair, *very* fat people, *very* grey people, but it was no
use. We were irrefutably the oldest people on the boardwalk.

This morning, while he showers, I'm on the balcony in
my pajamas, watching as light prances on the ocean.
There are so many bright blue umbrellas below and
I'm breathing in this buoyant air and I just can't wait
to get back down there and play more Skee-Ball.
Fascinating that my heart still beats so fast.

PART 3
MATTERS OF THE HEART

LOVE IS A TERRIBLE, TERRIBLE THING

Love is a terrible, terrible thing.
It tosses us roses and flutes of champagne.
It waltzes and whirls us till we wonder where
we will land, but I'll tell you – it ain't lover's lane.
Why do we fall for Love's fancy disguise,
blind to its games and its bouts of intrigue?
It showers us over with *Rapture Galore,*
then crashes us down from pure battle fatigue.
If we fathomed the bleeding before the first stab,
Lord above, we'd hightail it, scared out of our wits,
but undone in our longings, we can't comprehend
that Love doesn't care if we're broken to bits.
And that is the reason I'm pacing this floor,
looking at you and then looking away,
sending off smiles which misfire in mid-air,
carefully guarding the words I might say.
We're both of us quaking up high on this wire,
caught in a shudder, in fear for our lives.
Kiss me just once and I'll splinter, I'll die.
To let go is the lunacy no one survives.
Love is the thing to avoid at all cost!
But oh, come and kiss me. We're already lost.

THE JUMP

Hunched over on that bench like a wet dog,
you wore a brown sweatshirt and were dismal.
There were 12 of us sitting on the deck,
staring out to sea. A blowy hush of gold and
sky swept us, and there was chilled white
wine, mussels dug from the shore, bread and
cheese and laughs that rose and fell like
sighs through the thin dune grass.

You rose and lumbered down the path to
the cliffs, sending off puffs of gloom like an
old mushroom. You reached the edge and
looked out, drawing on your cigarette, cradling
your glass of wine. You might have been some
Lord in a crimson robe, commanding fleets.
I might have joined you as your Lady, but we
no longer fed on illusion.

After lunch, I, too, made the journey to stand
before the cliffs. Oh – instantly my eyes were
yanked down, *ambushed* by the rocks below,
huge rocks clawed and slathered by the waves.
Sea-dragons leapt from the spray, yowling: *Fly!*
Wind wrenched at me: *Jump!* Those slung-out
rocks – drunk and rollicking – bellowed: *Now!* And I

spun around, sprinted back up the path. Didn't
want to spoil the picnic. Well, they'd think I'd
killed myself. And I couldn't explain I was only
succumbing to sea-dragons. I sat beside
you on the bench. Our bodies slurped at the air

between us, groping for a link, a knot. I hissed
to you, not looking in your eyes, "My God...
I wanted to jump." You said, "I know. I did, too."

Oh, we had a bad love. It blew out so fast, left
us hanging by our toes, mortified. Yet there was
this one thing, wasn't there? This twisted bond,
this dalliance with death. Together, for a moment,
we were both plumb-crazy.

HAPPINESS

Once a young man brought me
a china bowl filled with raspberries.
I had overslept. It was a late-morning
breakfast just for me. We sat on a cool
summer terrace and I poured cream
over the raspberries till they floated.
I have never forgotten this.

The young man lived on a farm and the
raspberries had been plucked that very
morning from bushes in his field. The
terrace was beflowered and pristine, one
side fenced off to keep the cows away.
But how lovely when they moseyed over,
resting their brown and white heads atop
the wooden fence. Off and on, they mooed
like crooning dinosaurs.

The young man, who had risen at dawn, sat
very close and stared at me. He laughed.
He had never been in love before and it was
a wonder to him to sit and watch me eating
raspberries. One huge tear slid down his
cheek and he did not wipe it off.

Happiness can be so hard to take.

BUBBLES

Our children run together on the grass
with bubble-pipes and fingers that stretch
to pluck one huge bubble as it falls in the
plum air. You and I drink wine and watch.
My husband barbecues the chicken.
Your wife, the doctor, drinks gin as she
nurses a two-week old baby.

She knows how I loved you when we were
both 22. "Thank God you loved him first,"
she says. "You made him bearable." My
husband would prefer the whole topic to be
dropped, but he turns the chicken, acquiescent.

I remember you arriving for our affair,
standing in the doorway with a bag full of
wine, strawberries and three brand new
Chopin albums. You announced,
"Well, I've spent all my money!"
You shook your head at me, ruefully,
as if I'd dogged you all the way, beaten you
upon the head, shouting: Buy Chopin! Buy fruit!

And I remember the night you got down
on your knees, tears in your eyes, begging me
to stop making you laugh. It was the laughing
made you love me. And you didn't really
want to love me. And I kept on, ruthlessly,
getting funnier and funnier.

It's growing dark. My husband and I stare

at your wife's breast, intrigued that the baby's
face has now disappeared. Suddenly
you're up and running in the field with your
son and our two daughters – they're tying
you up in a jumprope and you're squealing.
Now they drag you past the Maple tree.
The moon is rising through the sky in a blur,
and we are four adults, 38 years old, all a
little fat, a little drunk, a little baffled not to be
the ones blowing bubbles.

I THOUGHT OF YOU TONIGHT

I thought of you tonight – a jolt so quick,
it frightened me. How can you still be here
inside me like a drug I cannot kick?
These sudden hits of you don't disappear.
I see your face, that slightly jaded smile,
and still I hear your voice, so lush, so low.
My God – we were so reckless! For a while
I turned into someone I didn't know.
I thought I'd killed you off! I need you *gone*.
How do I break from what I can't resist?
I've been your trick, your party doll, your pawn.
Oh God, the *worst* of you is what I've missed.
Turn up the lights. Lay down the violin.
It isn't love. It's lust that caves us in.

WATERBIRDS

In my dream I was dead. I was
flying. I was beautiful, sailing by
night, shadowing you through narrow
cobbled lanes as you loped from
church to church, gasping like a stag,

praying not to love me, and reaching
each altar, you would whirl back to see
me hovering above, silent, intractable.
The rose windows burned upon your face.

Your last vast church was rocketing
with echoes of my breath, each breath
urging you to die into me, and as you
met my eyes, your breath released
and you lifted. We swept toward each
other like waterbirds gliding under
rafters. A thousand candles were lit

beneath us, wavering, warming our
wings, as we drifted through a window,
melting, dropping to an earth soft with
tulips. And you spoke. You said only,
"Oh, you move me…"

MOMENTS OF ALMOST DYING

Tosca is on the radio.
We are driving north and *Tosca* has
taken off on a wild drunk, flooding
the car. I open the window. Shadowed
hills loom. Cold air pummels in, throttles
me back so I cannot help but look at you.
You are so pure, so unafraid of the music.

We lurch! We're turning east now
and your hand is lifting, buoying into
the music. Sudden sun crackles cross
the hills and I look at you, the light
flushing your face. The music's swelling.
Your eyes are thrilled. You tell me
Tosca's heart is breaking. The soldiers
are coming for her. Any moment now
she will jump from the castle parapet.
The music shudders, louder, shameless.
The road is rushing. Oh God, this awful,
awful music splits me open, makes me
want to die. If they would just stop singing!
If we were not at breakneck pace!
Tosca cries out, "Avanti a Dio!"
and leaps into the arms of God.

I look at you and you are luminous,
sated. All your life, you've let the
music take you and yet you haven't died.

But oh, how music betrays me, guts me,
thrusts way too deep and in the deep,

there is you and I cannot brawl with
my own heart. I do need you. You are
my love. I cannot look away.

DO YOU WANT TO DANCE?

We are the last to seat ourselves at table 29,
punctuated with scooped balls of butter, belled
radishes, plump rolls, crystal water goblets.
There is much nodding goes around the table while
the jewels of well-coifed ladies flutter in the
candlelight. He turns to me with a quick sigh
and says, "Do you want to dance?"

We dance. Feelings stumble cross his face,
forage through his eyes till he sighs again.
"I guess," he says, "I'm happy."
(Up his mother springs! *"God forbid!"*
Up above the dance floor with the
ghost of his father, both flailing arms,
howling *"God forbid you lose your job!*
You smash your car! The roof caves in!
Mortgage! Taxes! Kidney stones!") But
nonetheless, he has said it. And like some
vaulter on a slim golden pole, he is beautiful.

We sit again. The table has now become Edwardian,
full laden with veal chops, parslied potatoes, haricots vert.
The silky waiter dips down and purrs, "Red or white?"
Smiles cloy the air. Brocaded bodies lean into us,
hum down our throats like swarms of summer bees.
He turns to me with an ache in his eyes.
"Can we just go back and dance?"

We dance. Everyone else in the world clinks
and chews and chats. But we dance. He pulls
me into the grace of his shoulder. With the

saddest smile, he whispers, "I love my wife.
I love my children." He twirls me out and grabs
me back in again and his fear is glorious.

OPENING THE SHUTTERS

I watched you opening the shutters
as I lay in bed, not yet ready to face
the day. *Always* you open every shutter-
purposeful and quick – the moment you
see my eyes have actually opened.
And *always* it annoys me-
I'm not ready yet for all this light!

But today what came over me-
a thought blowing in, then taking root-
this is what you've done for 30 years,
pulled me from the comfort of my dark
into the light I must have to survive.
This is instinct for you.
Do you know that you keep me alive?

PART 4
HOME

CLOSETS

The question isn't: why does my dog run into the closet
during thunderstorms? The question is: why don't I join
her, sitting in the dark atop old boots and umbrellas,
waiting out the jags of lightning, whacks of thunder,
smacks of backfire from the street, the daily dread
of jets zinging cross Manhattan, the caustic dinners
blurred with red wine, the cracks of cold laughter,
the backs turned on what's no longer young?

There are things to be said for the closet or the bed,
the warm cape of madness, always one breath away.
My dog scurries deeper into the closet, head down,
legs quaking. She knows the score. Is it so judicious
that I try to quell my shakes and stand my ground?
Is it noble to brute one's way through betrayals?
Am I smarter than my dog lying here in the dark?
I don't know if I like the pack I run with.

T.J.

T.J. came in on the red-eye from San Francisco,
7 weeks old, a Cocker Spaniel with a blue
ribbon on his collar. The last words his
owner said were, "Yep, he's a frisky one."
When we walked T.J. through the door,
he attacked a metal trashcan. That was five
years ago. It was just a warm-up.

The doorbell rings and T.J. runs amok.
Delivery men vault into the air: "Does he
bite?!" We say "No!" and then we pray.
Elevator time is always daunting. That woman
on the 6th floor used to hiss, "He's *vicious,*"
till the day I raised my eyebrows and said,
"But don't you know? It's *seizures.* He has
Chronic Idiotitis of the brain." "Oh dear," she
murmured, as he flailed away. "How tragic."
I nodded. She added, "Poor dear thing."
I said, "Well, we don't need to go that far."

T.J. also loathes every other dog on the street.
He barrels forth, head-on, *hysterical.* One day
a dogwalker reared back in terror: "What's
happening?!" she screamed. "My God," I said.
"I don't *know!* It must be something he ate!"

Well, it's only fair to mention something good
about T.J.: he's embarrassed when he farts.
Also, when my husband comes home from
work, T.J.'s reverence knows no bounds.
He bends his knees to pee upon the bed.

There are days, I'll admit, when I yell "Shit, why am I stuck with this utter fool?!" Because I know I'm gonna die with this dog. When I'm lying on my deathbed, he'll be nosing through the wastecan, chewing on the foil from an old Hershey's kiss.

And just when I'll be thinking all this – here he comes down the hall with his beloved old ratty Bugs Bunny rabbit hanging from his mouth. He plops it down in my lap, sighs, and looks at me with an expression that can only be interpreted as "You are the love of my life." I sigh back at him and whisper, "Yeah, I love you, too..."

WEEKENDS WITH THE HUSBAND

He's got time on his hands. Two days to prowl the
house, hissing... *Use a coaster... Why's this light on?...*
(And it's breath-taking when he lasers in on cardboard
boxes: *Crush them FLAT before they go into the trash!!*)
Uh-oh. Here he comes with a sponge. Never a good
sign. He heaves down, scrubs dog pee from the rug,
muttering at this betrayal, up again now, heading
through the bedroom, stops, turns, flings into my office,
pounces: *The dust ruffle's filthy! No, of course you
wouldn't notice! No, I'm quite sure you've never even
THOUGHT about dust ruffles your whole entire life!*

I close the door.

I read today that Raymond Carver died at 50. I am 46.
I am going to write today, the next day, every day.
I will demand my time, my solitude, I will insist-

SHIT! I DON'T BELIEVE IT! Apparently he's yelling
at a water filter. They sent the wrong size water
filter for the fridge. Now the dog is barking!
Everybody hates this water filter!

And that's when, like the Trevi Fountain, this poem
springs up into my mind! My pen begins to scrawl.
First, a title. I could call it "The Hellish Water Filter."
No. "Dust Ruffles?" Sounds a bit too elegant. Or-
Wait! I've got it! "Man with a Sponge!" Or does that
sound too much like a confused James Bond?
Anyway I'll start with "He's got time on his hands,"
cause he only does this shit on weekends.

Man, this is gonna be great-

The door opens. He stands before my desk, bereft:
There's absolutely nothing here for lunch except
a can of corned beef hash.

And so I fry him some eggs with his hash and he
smiles his thanks because I've rescued him from a
day of ceaseless, sordid, staggering domestic blows.
I smile back because I got this poem.
Seems to me a reasonable trade-off.

I find I am leaning toward "Man with a Sponge..."

DRIVING HOME FROM SNOW WHITE

It is that hour of falling darkness.
Golden light puffs down behind a farmhouse.
A deer, grazing, pausing by the road,
blends into bush and in a flash, the gold
has mellowed, flushing the sky. You see?
If you look away, even for an instant, the sky
has swerved. The light's forever shifting.

We are driving our four year old home
from *Snow White and the Seven Dwarfs*.
The wicked queen has been smashed by
a rock in the rain. Snow White has kissed
the dwarfs goodbye and been side-saddle
led into pastel hills by this very lovely man.

"Look!" We gasp together, my husband and I.
We are crossing the reservoir, a stretch
of silver shuddering to pink at the edge
of the sky. Trees lash up around the lake,
amazed. We do not dare to look away.
"Look!" we call to our daughter, driving on,
singing the songs, naming the dwarfs, while
she sleeps, buckled fast in her car seat.

As we turn into our dirt drive, a skunk
waddles quickly underneath our barn,
which is her home. Oh so quietly, so
she will not spray us, we move from the
car, carrying our child, her head droopy,
eyes bleary. And as we near the house,
my husband sings, "I'm wishing..." And

softly, I echo, "I'm wishing..." And we both
sing "for the one I love..." And we laugh.
Bronze light spills across the field.
For a moment, we just stand by the door,
staring out, very still. We know soon the sky will
swerve, so soon. The light's forever shifting.

THE SHOE

-Nola, come here.

-I'm not available right now.

-Nola, you better get in here. I mean it.

-I'm sorry. I'm just not up to it.

-Nola! Now! *(Child approaches bathroom. Slowly.)* Kindly leave your wagon in the hall.

-You know you shouldn't shout on a Jewish holiday.

-*What?* This isn't a Jewish holiday.

-How do you know?

-And you're not Jewish.

-Well, neither are you!

(Confused mother takes a pause, then once more into the breach)

-All right, Nola. I want you to look in the toilet. Take a good look and then tell me what you see.

-Daddy's shoe.

-Precisely. And who put Daddy's shoe in the toilet?

-Daddy.

-Okay, all right, okay. Let's assume that Daddy did put his shoe in the toilet-

-He did.

-Fine, fine. But *why* would Daddy do that?

-Because he hates that shoe.

-Nobody hates a shoe!

-Mommy, you really shouldn't shout on-

-Today is *not* a holiday, not Jewish, not Christian, not
Buddhist, not any day except a *day*, plain old normal day
and if I'm shouting-

-You are.

-Okay, young lady – how would you like to reach in there and
remove Daddy's shoe. That's not a question.

-It sounded like one.

-Enough, Nola! Take the shoe out of the toilet. *You* put it in, *you*
take it out.

(*Child thinks*)

-Umm... I'm guessing that *somebody* in this apartment – probably
Daddy – by mistake got magic marker on the shoe and couldn't
get it off-

-Let's pause right there for a moment, shall we? Why would
Somebody-Probably-Daddy be drawing on the shoe?

-Well, I don't think this person was drawing. I think maybe this
person was doing a science experiment.

-Uh-huh. You want to elaborate on that?

-Well, to see if somebody could make a brown shoe be black.

-Uh-huh. Go on.

-So then if the person – probab-

-Probably-Daddy, right.

-Umm-hmm. So maybe this person got nervous about it maybe
not being a *good* science experiment because the black magic
marker wouldn't come off-

-and so the person dumped the shoe in the toilet and kept
flushing it, hoping that-

-No, no. First the person tried the sink and then also the bathtub. So then...

-She tried the toilet.

-She must have done that. But then the toilet stopped flushing, so-

-Are you telling me that you also broke the *toilet?*

-No. That was the shoe.

-All right. I am now going to count to ten and-

-Why?

-count to ten, take several deep breaths and then I'm going to just sit back and enjoy watching you take the ruined shoe out of the broken toilet.

-What about flesh-eating disease?

-...*What?*

-You were telling Daddy about this lady who fell into a pond and got the flesh-eating disease and the germs killed her. Didn't you say that to Daddy? I heard you say that to Daddy. If somebody falls into a pond-

-This is not a pond! This is a toilet!

-I thought you were going to count to ten.

(*Mother takes the dripping-wet shoe out of the toilet. Mother and Child examine the shoe. Then:*)

-Mommy, you look very sad.

-Yes. (*Fixated on shoe*) It's an existential sadness...

-I don't know what that means. (*Pause*) Are you sad more about the shoe or the toilet? (*Pause*) Or flesh-eating disease.

-I have no idea what to do with this shoe...

-I'll tell you. You should throw it away and then you tell Daddy that a burglar came in and took the shoe. And he had a gun.

-Inspired, Nola. I'll also say he wore a cape and had a wooden leg.

-And maybe say it was him broke the toilet. Okay, I gotta go now.

-Having a busy day, are you?

-Umm-hmm. And Mommy, don't worry about your shirt. I'm sure you can clean it off where the black magic marker is dripping all over it, but if you can't, you can just throw that away, too.

I LOVE YOU SO MUCH. Bye-Bye!

PIE

One night we just started talking about pie.
I said to him, "Name your five favorites."
Straight-out he said, "Cherry. That's my first.
But..." He cocked his head. "I do love Peach."
"That's okay," I said. "It can be a tie. *My* first-"
"Of course," he murmured, "there's always
Blueberry." He was now suspended in thought.
"Right," I said. "So we'll get back to you.
My first is Chocolate Walnut Pie. Served hot
or cold. Second definitely: Pecan Pie."
"Hmm." He shook his head. "Not my favorite."
"Well," I said, "you're not from Baltimore."
We both, after some rumination, passed
on Pumpkin and felt bad about that.
I continued. "Lemon Meringue – Oh my God!"
His eyes flared. "*What? What's wrong?!*"
I gripped his arm. "Remember that lobster
place in Menemsha? The Homeport! Remember
how every night they had like ten different pies?
And – oh, wow, their Key Lime was-" He pounced!
"Key Lime! That's my new number one or-...
unless..." Slowly a silence fell. "I guess,"
he said, "I just like pie." I met his eyes.
"Yeah, me, too. Pretty much all pies. Except
for Rhubarb. I mean, who *are* these people
who eat Rhubarb pie?"

It was at this point, he turned to me and said,
"Do we have any pie?"
But he already knew – we *both* knew-
there was no pie in the house, only those

Stop & Shop cupcakes I bought with the
stupefying red and turquoise icing.
"We'll go get some pie tomorrow," I said.
"What kind?" he asked. Another silence fell.
We looked at each other, lost, adrift.
"Okay, so…" I smiled. (He does depend on me
for glass-half-full.) "Name your five favorite…
Cakes!" Instantly I knew this was the wrong
tack to take, pitting cake against pie. "Pastas!"
I said. "Five favorite pastas? Or we could do…
Dairy Products?" It was no good. Reader,
heed my tale. Reader, take my warning:
Once you've done pie… there is no turning back.

SITTING HERE, READING ABOUT COWS

I am sitting here, reading about cows.
Apparently cow farts are destroying our planet.
I put my feet up to think.
Oh, come on.

My daughter walks through the room.
"It's true," she says, shaking her head, rueful.
It seems I am not up on my zoology

Well, this is just awful.
All day long the image lingers - cows
whooshing gas, toxic explosions of
methane or whatever.
But why specifically cows?
Why not buffalo? Or horses?
Or very big pigs?

Look out! Here he comes- Lenny,
my daughter's hurtling dog - *thud!*
He's on my chest, hellbent to lick inside
my mouth. Indeed, dogs ignore protocol
and God knows dogs are expert farters,
so I ask you: why not *dogs?*

I love cows.
Did you know that they love music?
If someone plays a flute, a fiddle,
a guitar, cows come walking
through meadows, over hills
to form semi-circles, holding stock
still, just to hear the music.

I think we need to blame the farts
on someone else, like, for example,
the Royal Family or
Congress or
the Akron Symphony Orchestra,
the entire cast of *The Young and the Restless*,
the Girl Scouts of America and their cookies,
the Four Horsemen of the Apocalypse.

Just not cows.

ELIZA AT 6

Like bone china, like a fragment of
shell, tossed and pearly on the sand,
she is translucent. In her photographs
she is my ghost, so lovely I have to
laugh. I tremble at my half-fleshed bird.

She dances for me, head cocked down,
eyes fixed and somber, hips in a swivel.
Legs straddle air, fingers rub in soundless
snaps. If I watch too closely, she will stop.

Silently she becomes a collector.
Her room reels with rhinestones,
postage stamps, butterflies and
rocks. Last week she came home from
school with a gift for me: a broken
chunk of city sidewalk. Mysterious,
she smiled. Obedient, I placed this
slab of Manhattan on my bed table.

This is my thin child, my daughter
with her secrets, my veteran of divorce
and alternating holidays. Coming home
from Easter with her father, she climbed
off the train, worn and weary, stood
in Penn Station with her fingers tight
upon her gay little Easter basket.
Home again, fuming at the world,
she came to find me. Eyes sizzling,
she handed me a golden egg.

She takes no bears to bed.
I wander into her dark room and sniff her
open perfume bottles, hear her shushed
breath. Her silky white nightgown gives
off a sheen like the moon. And always,
even in sleep, she seems distant as
the stars. In her dreams (or is it in
mine?) she becomes the pristine
ballerina atop a music box, dancing,
dancing round and round, turning,
turning, always turning the other cheek.

MOMMY

My day is the doll on the floor,
grape juice sprayed on the linoleum,
and the hulk of myself I lug from
room to room. Oh, my daughter,
my crazy thing with thin bangs,
you plunk on the floor with your
fur mouse. You shake him and say,
"What's the matter, Mouse? God's sakes!"
And then your head tosses up to me,
groping for that monster love I
must give in doses, hourly,
to stem the fears.

You crawl across my papers.
"Don't worry, Mommy." You pat.
"It's going to be allllright," you say.
When my head falls back, you pull at me.
"No, no, get up. Don't sleep." But I am
so heavy. There is so much, so many
things, the soup to cook, the pots to
clean, blocks to pile, small crumpled
shirts to stack, I am so heavy, dying.
"No, Mommy. Get up, Mommy!"

You cling me over, drag me up. We spin.
"I want to dance, Mommy! Mommy, *dance!*"
And we tumble on the stuffed dogs and
rabbits. Leaden chill turns in my belly.
There has been no sun for months.
You must have air. I must give you light!
"I want to sing, Mommy. *Sing!*"

I sing, you sing, your yellow hair rolling
on your neck, wispy, pretty. You are so
pretty. "Sing!" It grows dark and we are
tangled on this floor, loving, lost, sapped.
You kiss me. You watch. So quiet now.

"Mommy." You wait, your hand a bird
on my throat. "Mommy, don't you know
I love you?" And then you smile.
Oh, there is amazing music in this pain.

NOTES ON A DEPRESSION

You know, I hide in it. I burrow, drifting
deep into down pillows and if
doorbells ring – well, how can I hear?

When it's raining, it holds
me, enfolds me. Faintly, it
whispers: *you don't ever have*
to step out that door again.

Why would you call this pain? Nothing
hurts. It's only very quiet. And I won't
believe it's a prelude, a sneak-peek
into the deep dark art of dying.

No, mine is drowsy, slow and dumb,
a living thing I slide inside, where I can
breathe in endless falling, falling snows
and feel the trace of God's sad smile.

HOOFBEATS

I write till 1:00 or 2:00 or 3:00 or dawn-
an outlaw's life, yes. Still, it's what I choose.
Why not be Jesse James with pistols drawn
and gallop through some rhythms?
(or some blues...)
Come, pen and paper, lighter, cigarette-
let's revel in my idiot's delight.
I know one day I'll have to pay. Not yet!
I need my restless world. I need the night.
Yes, other women sleep in pastel beds,
their faces soft with moisturizing creams.
No huffing horses buck inside their heads.
They sleep in peace. No desperado dreams.
I'll never know that respite, but why cry?
I'll feel the pound of hoofbeats till I die.

PART 5
MOM & DAD

HEY! MOM AND DAD ARE BACK!

It's Fall! Time for the visit! It's going to go really well!

THE FIRST HOUR

Dad is marking his territory like a dog. Down goes his pipe,
pipe tobacco, pipe cleaners, books – an Agatha Christie,
a biography of Winston Churchill and his Columbia Viking
Desk Encyclopedia, which he takes with him everywhere for
resource purposes when he does his New York Times Double
Crostic puzzles (which are attached to his clipboard to which
his two personal pencils are also clipped). He then proceeds
to check out the bar ("You're low on gin") and lecture my
husband, as always, for not drinking enough (to which my
mother, as always, says "Never trust a man who doesn't drink")
and Dad caps off the hour by looking at my dog and muttering,
"He's a miserable animal." I could possibly take umbrage
but just then my father turns and shuffles off down the hall
and Mother says, "Poor dear fellow – he can't bend his knees
anymore." She adds "Your father is a saint."

COCKTAIL TIME

Holding her bourbon aloft, Mother clears her throat, summons
up her terrifying memory bank and proceeds to play the room.
(Up first – a melodic selection from First Grade P.S. 64:)
Tell me what's as red as a rose, as blue as the sky, as white as
the snows: Hurrah! Hurrah! Tis America's beautiful flag!
(A sip of Wild Turkey and let's jump to a high school anecdote:)
Carroll Klinglehoffer wrote my name on his tennis shoes.
I just ignored him. (Skipping generations:)...*that New Year's*
Eve party when we hung gold balls from the ceiling and Walter
Gunst hit his head on a ball. Well, he was way too tall a man
and – Ah, now her hearing aid's gone dead so she can't hear us

trying to get a word in and just as I'm about to hurl myself out
the window, she tosses in a jewel I actually have never heard
before. (This time it was that in 1952 in Provincetown, she saw
the Northern Lights and had a panic attack.) Now my father
wanders in with his gin, sits in my husband's leather chair and
says, "Your mother is a remarkable woman."

By the way, both my parents will totally outlive me.
I'll be dying, they'll be having Mint Juleps.

DINNER TIME

So for 3 days I've been cooking! Carrot-Ginger soup!
Fried Chicken! Sausage-Cheddar Biscuits! Lemon
Meringue Pie! Brandied Peaches! I impress myself.
And now, standing here, stirring soup, I am even more
impressed with myself that I do not reach for a gun when
Mother says, "At any rate, I'm glad we don't have to eat
take-out Chinese like the last time," and you should note
the last time they ate take-out Chinese in my home was
7 years ago when I'd just given birth and apparently almost
died. (One nurse said *"Oh, we're so glad you made it!"*)
Finally home and in bed *(and alive)* with a newborn baby
clutched in my arms, we said to the new grandparents,
"Mind if we get Chinese?" I continue to stir the soup,
taking deep breaths and making myself remember that
the better part of valor is…what? I can't remember what.
But I'm doing it. Lots of valor.

MORNING

They were catching an early train, so they'd said "Don't
get up," but I'm thinking to myself, "You know what?
Everything considered, it's all gone fairly well, basically,
right?" And so I rise. I greet Mother in the kitchen and she

coos, "Next time you go to the market, do buy some
marmalade. You've run out of marmalade, but that's all
right. We found a dab of grape jelly and we did have some
toast, but of course there was no coffee and no English
Muffins for your father, but that's all right," with which I
yank forth the fresh pack of English Muffins, hoist the
coffee to the air, and brandish the Blueberry Preserves.
"Oh," she says, sniffing slightly, "we didn't want that
Blueberry." I do not say: "WHAT THE F*$#&% IS WRONG
WITH THE BLUEBERRY?!" She looks askance at the
pack of English Muffins and says, "We of course thought
they would be in the breadbox." I do not say: "NOT ONE
BLOODY SOUL ON EARTH STILL HAS A BREADBOX!"
Now, noticing I'm not breathing, she gives me a pat. "No
matter," she says. "No matter." And look – Dad has just
joined us! With a saintly hand on my shoulder, he says,
"My dear, you really do need to keep a box of kleenex
in that bedroom. And might I suggest that you get a few
extra pillows?" Hold on, hold on, they're almost

AT THE DOOR

Mother does a reprise of "No matter, no matter," and now I
am actively looking for a gun – there must be a gun – when I
see her stuff two scruffy raincoats into a tote-bag that says
"Hollins Lane Veterinary Clinic" and my father drags their
antediluvian suitcase out the door – schlumpf, schlumpf–
into the foyer and Mother shrugs at me and says, "Well,
here goes the Old Fart Express," and at this point, my
wrath fizzles off like helium from a balloon. You know, it's
just too hard to write off the good stuff.

So what they'll remember when they visit next year will be
no Kleenex, low on gin, no marmalade, the loathsome

Blueberry Preserves and the continuing presence of the
miserable animal.

That's the way it goes.
We never stop going apeshit to please our parents.
We never can please our parents.
Yep, that's the way it goes.

But if I ever do this – I tell my kids –
if I ever do this shit with marmalade:
throw me to the wolves.
Better yet – just shoot me.
(Think ahead: get a gun).

MOTHER AT 73

Mother takes her teeth out and then
comes in to see if I still love her. Barefoot,
she walks across our hall, pulling the ties
of her pink tumble-down bathrobe.
She leans against my doorway. She's
watching me. "I took my teeth out,"
she says, narrowing her eyes. I give her
back nothing but a fixed smile. She sniffs.
"Someday," she says, "you, too, will
have to take your teeth out." She pats
her hair. It is the color of moonshine.
She told me so.

This time, Mother brought me pink Rubrum Lilies,
plunged into a yellow bucket. They bounced
in the car all the way up the New Jersey Turnpike.
She brought a Smithfield ham and bourbon.
She sips the bourbon in my garden and tells
my little girl, "Listen, you – aging is very strange.
Do you think I *feel* the way I *look*?"
My little girl thinks, then shakes her head.
Mother says, "Of course not. Inside I'm a sylph.
A sylph. Look it up."

After dinner, Mother plays the piano.
She pumps the loud pedal like stepping on the gas
and says to me, "Remember Hurricane Hazel?
You were five. The lights went out. You danced
through the candles while I played a Swedish waltz."
Her smile is grand as she plays the Swedish waltz.
My little girl dances. Mother nods and says

her daily mantra: "You'll miss me when I'm gone."
And I grab up her words and her waltz
and the turn of her old, pretty head
and I shake away my fear like a dog.

THE DREAM MOTHER

In my fantasy, her face opens,
her voice swells and she says
"Tell me, honey. *Tell* me."
And I cry and she pats my hand.
(Even in fantasy, my mother
only knows how to pat a hand.)

I grew up in Sunshine Land. Oh,
the whimsy, the merry music,
golden glimmers, rosy, rosy light
whiffling down the halls...........
When the rains came, when the
colors melted and the music died
away, Mother waltzed on in her
own blind beauty.

If only she had heard me, seen me
stooping there in the rain – just once-

But the Dream Mother sees it all.
She walks in search of me. Lullabies
beat in her breast and when she
meets me in the hallway, she stops-
her face blooms with recognition.

YOU HAVE TO GO HOME

Mother, I stood in your blue bedroom, looking out
your latticed window to the garden below
where your azalea bushes blushed in the sun.
I heard your voice spring up from the terrace
like a girl's: "Hey, come on down here."
"Coming," I called.
But still I stood, suspended in your blue-room
smells: powder, painted wood, clean sheets,
library books. I fell upon your bed with a fist
in my belly, knowing a day will come

when I step into your bedroom and the feel
of you still lingers and – *here* is her sweater,
freshly tossed. In the bathroom – her neat piles
of white washcloths gently stolen from hotels.
Walk into the kitchen, see the sinkful of pots
not yet washed, the recipes tacked askew to
the walls, the cats' faces lifted, waiting to be
fed. She *must* be here, hand on hip, musing.
Try the garden – she'll be *there*, plucking weeds,
puffing on a cigarette, laughing, bright-haired…

I went to find you. What could I say?
We sat on the terrace, waiting out the hour till
I'd catch the train and leave you again.
"Oh, you're always leaving," you said.
"Well, I suppose you have to go home."
You kept chatting and sipped a coke.
The orange cat angled by, brushing against
your legs. You grabbed him up and sat him
on your lap – a proud child with a new toy.

The cat purred, rubbed his nose across your
cheek. "Otis is very happy right here,"
you said, and then, in confidence to Otis,
"In New York City, no one ever sees a rainbow."

You let me off at the train station and turning
back for a moment, I said to you, "Mother,
you really wish I was a cat, don't you?"
"Of course," you said. Off you sped in your
dusty red Toyota. I stood, suitcase in hand,
never quite knowing where to go.

SHE DOESN'T LIKE THE SKY

She looks out the window
and doesn't like the sky.

White. Mute.

She sits in a hospital room.
In the bed is her mother-in-law
(or father, mother. It changes
year to year, one or the other.)

A nurse passes by, and waves a
brisky hand. "Happy Thanksgiving!"

Yes, it is Thanksgiving Day
and she will give thanks. She
always does or else God will be
furious because she *eats*, has a
home, a *family,* she's *alive*, and
and how dare she *ever* open
wounds of her own?

How dare she mind sitting here,
holding the hand of her mother-
in-law (father, mother), wanting
nothing more in the world right
now than a book to read?!
Selfish! Callous!
Holding that thin, limp hand,
she looks out the window again
where the sole smudge of color
is a yellow mist of trees, so far off,
it blurs into the air. Her eyes

fasten on the steeple of a church-
white, white against the cold white sky.

She doesn't like the sky today.
So what?

Give thanks on Thanksgiving!
Heathen! Egotist! On your knees!

UNDAUNTED

He sits in his chair in his room and his room is
his world and his world is a blur, warm and dim.

Two doctors came to see him yesterday morning-
not to treat his illness but to share memories of work
from 40 years ago. There were several laughs-
those days he remembers – followed by his offer
of brandy and cigars. That was when the doctors rose
to say goodbye and he smiled. "I hope to see you anon."

Today his wife bustles in. She's wearing yellow.
"I like you in yellow," he says. She sits with him.
"Did you bring cookies?" he asks. She says,
"I will tomorrow." He nods. "You'll bring the cookies
tomorrow?" She nods. His son angles through the
doorway. "Good of you to come," he says. When his
daughter walks in, he points to his son and asks her,
"Have you two met? He's a delightful fellow."
When they all leave, he waves a courtly hand
and says, "Perhaps you'll come again."

The big male nurse Kenneth arrives to lift him from
his slump in the wheelchair. "How ya doin', Doc?"
He likes Kenneth and he loves Jackie, who has big
breasts and gives him hugs. Sometimes when he's
alone, he bellows, "Jaaaaaaackie!" If she doesn't
come, he loses patience, wheels himself into a
corner and is stuck. "Jaaaaaaaaackie!!!" When
Jackie comes, she says, "What're you doin' in the
corner, Dr. P?" He looks at her in surprise and then
they both laugh. Jackie asks, "Would you like to

hear your music?" He smiles. "Indeed," he says.
"Very good of you." She slips a tape into the player
and turns it on. It's him singing. Jackie always says,
"You sing so good," and he nods, raising one hand
to conduct, eyes adrift, agleam and his hand is his
scepter, lifting and dipping through lustrous air
as he sits on his throne in this kingdom where he
alone reigns, undaunted.

STAY

My father went into this bed,
a proud old horse. Now they've
got him on his side, tubes affixed,
here, there... His dignity has been
drained away and he reaches out
one white hand to me and says,
"Stay."

He's never said that to me before.

Nurses come and go like dragonflies,
buzzing, flitting, pricking, probing.
The pumps and bottles clink and
gurgle. Doctors pop in and out,
brief floating people, checking,
murmuring. Otherwise it is just
my father and I in this room, his
belly half-exposed, his arms blue
from being stuck, his eyes nearly
wet as he looks up at me.
"Stay."

There is no doubt I will stay.
This is my father. Together we rode
the ocean waves. Together we sang
Handel in the Congregational Church.
This is my own father, poured out here
like so much old tissue. I hold to his hand.

Neither he nor I thought this is what his
death would be – we saw something

more like keeling over, crashing into glass, shocking out. And I am still not sure. I am still waiting for my father to rise, to set off again through the wind, cheeks burning.

IDENTIFICATION

I never did the conventional thing, which really was called for here-
(a quick but moribund glance: "Yes, that's my father") because I was
transfixed on the death room, floated into it, leaving my brother in the
doorway (from which he never budged), traversed the thirty feet to
the chest-high table, began to circle, sweating suddenly with doubt
because what was smacked down there was the head of a ghoul,
a sheet pulled to its neck. I was meant to believe you were under it.
Wrapped like a mummy? Naked? Hands folded cross your chest?
(as in: Blessed are the peaceful who are actually dead.) And I kept
rounding that table, taking in grey skin pulled so fucking tight across
the bones of the face – was this man *hollowed out?* Why the pointy
chin, pinched white lips? And then my eyes drifted to your silver hair.
Looking up, I saw my tremulous brother, standing in the doorway with
the funeral man who held an impatient box of Kleenex. I shouted,
"Would you bring me scissors?" The funeral man balked. "Scissors,"
I repeated. After he'd decided I was not dangerous, he brought me
tiny fingernail scissors and I snipped off a lock of your hair, Dad, the
one part of you that refused to die, and then, closing my fist tight
around it, I walked away from the corpse, back the thirty feet to my
brother and the funeral man who proffered his box of Kleenex and
wanted me gone right away. I handed him back the tiny scissors.
"Yes," I said. "That is my father's body," and then I opened my fist to
show the silver curl. My brother looked away. The funeral man opted
for a hacking cough. I told him, "I'm going to put it in a locket and give
it to my mother."

When I gave the locket to my mother, she was perplexed.
"His hair?" she said. "You put his hair into this?"
She put it in a drawer.
And that was that.

AFTER WE'D TALKED 20 MINUTES, SHE SAID...

-...and I do think *you* might give *me* a call sometime when I'm just here with all these foreigners.

-Mother, they're not foreigners. They're American and at least ten of them are your friends.

-Just the same, I have nothing in common with them. Except for that woman Dotty who only has one arm.

-Mother, you could be friendless and homeless. Instead you live at Brookside which might just as well be a 4-star hotel, plus it has a swimming pool and a great library.

-What?

-I simply said that at Brookside you have-

-How was your trip to France?

-It was great. But we do have to eat dinner now, so –

-I wish I could go to France. I don't think I've been out of here since your brother took me to the shoe store a year ago and even then I couldn't find a pair of shoes that fit so I wear tennis shoes night and day.

-Mom. We really are about to sit down-

-Oh, you're always about to do something. That philosopher was here again, but he doesn't say much.

-He's a psychiatrist.

-I just do all the talking. He wants me to take another pill. The philosopher. But the other pill didn't do me any good.

-That's why he wants you to try a *new* one.

-What? You know, I got that bathing suit you bought
me but it's way too tight.

-It's a size 14. You said a size 12 or 14.

-Nevertheless. What's more, I'm not at all sure I want
to use that swimming pool. Everyone here is incontinent.

-Mom – don't you have to go eat *your* dinner?

-We eat dinner here very early. 5:30. Much too early.
I'll tell you another thing about this Assisted Living.
There are some people here who aren't all together.

-Uh-huh. Isn't there some tv show you'd like to watch
right about now?

-I already have on that Dr. Phil. He's a windbag.

-Mom, you know I'm coming down to see you in 2 weeks?

-If I'm still alive. The man down the hall dropped dead.

-Oh, I'm sorry. Was he a friend of yours?

-Heavens, no. He's a teetotaler.

-Well, he *was* a teetotaler.

-Exactly. And he never smiled at anyone.

-What made him drop dead?

-I don't know. I just know he dropped smack on the
floor in the exercise room. And then he was dead.
His name was Perkins.

-Mom, our dinner's going to get cold.

-What *is* it you're having that's so important?

-Pork chops.

-Ha! We had prime rib roast.

-Well, even though we'll have to gag our way through
the pork chops, I am going to get off now, okay?

-Maybe someday you'll actually have time to talk to me.

-Yes, maybe I will.

-And you just came back from France. And I'm here with Dr. Phil.

-Seriously, Mom.

-What should I tell the philosopher?

-Tell him you'll try the new pill.

-Are you still taking all those pills?

-Umm-hmm.

-Well, I can't see why.

-For anxiety, depression, p.t.s.d., o.c.d., panic attacks and chronic insomnia.

-Well, you should certainly be able to sleep at your age.

-Okay, so goodnight then, Mom.

-Dr. Phil is now talking to some woman and it says under her name "Terrified of Mirrors." Well, no wonder. She's not appealing in the least. He always has on unappealing people.

-*Why* do you *watch* him?

-Occasionally it's interesting. Last week he had on this Miss America who got pregnant and moved to Turkey, although I can't see why anybody would move to Turkey, let alone have a baby.

-Okay, so the update here is that we're all now sitting at the table.

-Oh, fine. Stop taking all those pills.

-Okay, Mom. But you just take whatever pills they give you now, okay?

-We shall see. Maybe tomorrow *you'll* call *me*

-That would be lovely. I'm so sorry we didn't have a chance to talk tonight.

-I suppose we talked a bit.

-Clocking in at 31 minutes.

-But you were making dinner, so that doesn't count. Next time we'll have an actual conversation. And remember-

-You're going to say the thing again, aren't you?

-Yes: You'll miss me when I'm gone.

SLAPDASH

I can picture you right now, Mother,
on the Menemsha bight, canvas
propped, palette dabbed with
Prussian blue, bouncing yellows.
SWOOSH! Your brush thrusts,
sky splurges into pink! Now a
riffling seaway and *FLICK!* A few
skiffy boats take sail and then
you step back, puff for a moment
on a menthol cigarette and – *Hmmm…*
to the right – a fishing shack? (Next
idea is bubbling in.) *A shingled little*
shack… At the door – several cats,
waiting for some fish and *ZAP!* It's on to-

-the next canvas! And the *NEXT*, one
vision toppling upon another, nothing
ever quite finished, not quite, slap
and dash, move on to the *NEXT!*
Here's a house wondering why it still
has no windows. A child waits in vain
for some shoes. A lady in her garden
is irate – you never gave her ears!
She'll just have to cope. NEXT!
Oh, Mom you waltzed your way
through life like an endless gala,
thumbing your nose at the world.

(Once she attacked the kitchen floor:
FLING, SPLASH, out sprung the
mottled purples, swabs of ivory.

She was so pleased with her Jackson
Pollack kitchen, only slightly daunted
by the fact that all our shoes stuck
to the floor.) **MOVE ON!**

How you hated those last years,
Mother, muzzled by 98, 99, 100,
your mind grown feathery, smiles
snuffed out. Oh, the second you
died, how you flew! My God-
a **GUST!** I still clenched your hand.
"Mom?" I felt you pitching off that
stale old body and I waited for a
goodbye – one ghostly hand to
graze my face. No! Off you tore!
Cut-and-Run! Glamorous again,
cavorting into God-knows-where!
You wouldn't care! You were simply
mad to wing into the **NEXT**, your
paintbrush extended to the sky.

PART 6
THE GROWN-UP

30 MILES OUT TO SEA

I. THE NIGHTMARE

And once more the nightmare comes rattling in and I'm back
on the streets which are always deserted except for city
buses huffing by with no faces in the windows and then–
wham – the sirens start: *Whoop-Whoop-Whoop, Wah-ooo,
Wah-ooo, EEEE-ee, EEEE-ee,* careening, crescendo,
decrescendo, and now, folks, here's the main attraction:
a parade of smile-less men and women, marching single-file,
and bringing up the rear, like Hamlin's rats, are the children,
their eyes pip-popping out above their masks. I watch them
all go trudging down the smutty subway steps when suddenly
one smile-less man leaps out of line, rips off his mask and
I see he's foaming at the mouth. Then others leap. It's a
posse! Fury builds, all of them driven quite mad by the
sirens, ceaseless, screaming *EEEE-eee, EEEE-eee,* and
now they're boiling, walloping their way through the dark
tunnels till they burst up out of manholes, and rifles sprout
like extra limbs, rifle shots shrilling, shrilling-

-and I can't remember – sometimes that's where the dream ends?
Other times my brain decides to swish in pretty things like
raindrops on roses and whiskers on kittens – you know, just to
hush it up. Still, I know it keeps playing sub strata, and it will
return and I'll keep waking in a shudder, mumbling to myself,
"It's okay, you're okay, breathe, take a breath," and "Thank you,
God, thank you for letting me be here, 30 miles out to sea."
I am safe on this island where I believe only 4 have died.
Maybe 5? Over there, thousands die every day while I'm here
in the bright autumn air, walking down the dirt road, beside
the clear pond and, quite honestly, my safety overrides most

of my survivor's guilt. Of course I feel guilty admitting that.

II. THE WALK

So I'm walking down the road and lined up on either side are
the goldenrods, still tossing and beating at each other, refusing to
take part in the Fall. The wind heaves and a drove of seabirds
comes careening in just above my head, *so close*. God, this wind-
knocking me off-balance till I have to laugh – you know, a *jumpy*
laugh. And then the wind blusters me seaward and Good Lord!
Look at these whitecaps today, jerking askew, breaking into
shards of silver, toppling into waves which thwack the shore.
And I'm pulled closer, *closer* to the sea, my boots sinking into
sand as I climb a sand dune, dune grass whipping at my jeans,
and when I hit the crest of the dune – *oh wow!* I mean: *Wow! Oh,*
this is not your everyday ocean, folks! *No, no, no.* This ocean's
hellbent on havoc! Watch it hacking shells to bits, shattering
sea glass, gorging on the beach! Once long ago-

yes – Remember? That day we swam out too far – my cousin
Ann and I – suddenly sucked into a riptide and we would
have died, boiled alive, but for the two men who swam out
to save us. We thanked them and thanked them, called
them our guardian angels and never saw them again.

But it's like that now – ravenous waves thrashing away
at the sand dunes till the dunes begin to crumble, but I'm
okay, up here so high, an untouchable, free to gulp down the
mad clean smell of the sea, to know – *No, WHOA!* Another heave!
The wind keeps whomping in and now the sand springs,
stings my cheeks, gravels my eyes and I ask myself: Why in
God's name are you still standing here inside this yowl?!

So – okay. Enough. I've proven my point. I turn my back on the sea, race along the path to my house which is now enfolded by a slow fog. Perfect. Respite. Inside my house, the air is soft, the heat is on. Good. I lie down. I do hear the flap of a shingle rattling off into the wind. I do hear the squalling, the bawling of the wind outside, but note that there are no sirens here, no plague strafing my island.

III. THE PLAGUE

Is the world truly on its last gasp? March 2020 – life stopped.
Like a pistol shot. Like Sleeping Beauty when she pricked
her finger on the spinning wheel and *Zing!* Everyone in the
castle froze midair – the cook with his spoon still raised,
the laundress with her hands sunk in soapy water, the king
and queen, mouths open, set to scream at each other,
and, just like that, all of them – paralyzed. For 100 years. And
what of us? Will endless plagues keep sneaking in, year after
year, plunging us ever deeper into the Bible, into Apocalypse,
Armageddon? Even now, 30 miles back to the mainland,
hundreds of thousands are shrouded off into beds but there
are *no more beds*, no more cold, cold trucks for the bodies.
4,500 dead yesterday. *How can that be?!* And the nurses are
crying in the stairwells, then returning with gloved hands and
plexiglass faces to stroke the cheeks of those who ask,
"Am I going to die?"
"No," say the nurses. "You're not going to die,"
and when they die, it's on to the next pale and bewildered face.
"Am I going to die?"

And my nighttime brain now refuses to swish in *whiskers
on kittens.* I lie sleepless, becoming one of them, gasping,
"I can't breathe!" Sedated, paralyzed, tube jammed down my
throat, flipped on the bed lest my lungs cave in. But I'm certain
sedation wouldn't work on me. Paralyzed, yes, but conscious,

panicked, unable to shoot out a hand or cry, *"No! Stop!"*
And all I'd see would be the desperate eyes of doctors, nurses
bolting by in rubbered gowns en route to the ones who've been
selected to live, and all alone, I'd hear the sound of my machines,
the *whoosh-whoosh-hiss...* 9,000 dead today, 13,000, 23,000-
How can there be this many people?!
Aren't we running out of people?
Won't it soon be my turn?
No, no. What I must do is stay safe, stay here and write, write
poems, more and more poems. Someone in the future might
stumble upon them and comprehend the stark indifference of
this plague, its cyclonic gorging on human lives.
Who's next?
No, the best I can do is thank the Lord for my warm bed
on this safe island where I'm –

IV. THE WIND

-jack-knifed from my bed! It's the wind! Oh, it batters
at my windows, drags me out the door, wrenches back my
head till I see too many stars – like shivs, they pierce the dark!
This wind – it *seethes* into my bones, rasps down my neck,
"You smug and stupid woman." It gives my hair a yank and
jeers, "*Angels*?" It laughs, twanging me round and round like
an unstrung doll. "*You got a warm bed, that right?*" It cracks up.
It's having such fun with me. It slams me down. "Gee, I think
the plague *has* run out of people! Whada'ya know! It *is* your
turn!" It pins my shoulders. I can't move but I cry out, "I'm not
meant to die yet – I have work to do!" The wind's in stitches.
"Oh, yeah! I forgot. You're the hope of the future. Go write
your heart out, Peaches. Whatever." And It hoists me up,
barrels me to the beach! I begin to weep. The wind snickers,
"You smug and stupid woman," drops me hard on the sand,
then buzzes off, too disgusted to stick around. It dumps me like

so much excrement atop the shattering sea glass and the
sad, sad shells hacked to bits. But *no. No, no.*
Who listens to a lunatic wind? I will not. I'm going to walk
this beach in my bare feet, in my nightgown, hair unfurling,
swirling. The sea gnaws the sand. The sand melts beneath
my bare feet, the sea bursts – oh no, it soaks my pretty
nightgown. The sea *whoops! Whooshes!* Crescendo,
decrescendo! But I'm safe here on the edge of the world.
There is nothing between me and the coast of Portugal!
Only ocean, ocean, ocean! And here we have fog, always
a shrouding fog so no one can breach our island!
Not a boat, not a plane!
We are – *guess what*? Locked down! Literally locked down!
And here no one asks
"Am I going to die?"
And here I will stay with my melting feet, my seaweed hair.
"It's okay, you're okay," says God, "Take a breath. Breathe.
Come and walk with me beside the still waters. Let us drink
raindrops on roses. You and I are 30 miles out to sea,
30 miles away from the sweat and the shudder." He takes
my damp hand but all we do is stand and stare at the sea.

THE GROWN-UP

This hand on my husband
    is for being 13 and aching to be kissed
This flung open window
    is for the smell of cafeterias and locker rooms
This house of rolling books
    is for 2 English teachers, namely:
    Miss Barge who had never heard of Edward Albee
    Mrs. Gunderson who shamed me for reading Salinger
This lazing sleep till noon
    is for logarithms at 9:00 a.m.
This army jacket and Arizona boots
    are for madras skirts and circle pins
These breasts falling free
    are for:" Why do *you* need a bra?"
    Right. I don't.
These days of shutting doors when *I need them shut*
    are for having to always LIGHT UP THE ROOM!
These moments in the studio, recording songs,
    are to salute age 8, sitting alone on the grass,
    writing poems
That gentle man on the ship who said "You're beautiful"
    wipes out that boy in his car who shouted, "Hey, Ugly!"
And this poem
    is for my neighbor Rick, the lawyer, as he stood
    in the check-out line at the grocery store,
    watching a boy beg his mother for a Snickers
    and when the mother's back was turned, he whispered
    to the boy, "I can have *anything* I want."

5 HAIKU

Who can sleep at night
when the snow comes whipping down?
I'm at the window!

I've seen fire burning
inside the old Maple tree.
Can't tell anyone.

All those stars up there,
aglow, aglow every night-
don't they get restless?

I've stopped climbing down
the stairs. My head whirls. Should I
tell him I'm in love?

Last night you were there.
To hear your voice was like a
jolt of breaking glass.

THE DANCE

Blow the smoke from the room.
Drain the scotch from the rocks.
No more dancing on the tables,
no more shadows to box.

Yank the gust from the wind.
Douse the stars in the skies.
No more turning up the music,
no more urge in our eyes.

When we grow up, must we give up the heat,
beat a flustered retreat,
run from the dark sweet dancing
that set our souls astir?
Do you remember when we let down our guard,
and no holds were barred?
How beautiful when we didn't know
exactly who we were.

Strip the rip from the tides.
Hush the trembling air.
God, how did we lose the art
of living life on a dare?

Can't we bring back the music?
Let the sound ricochet!
We were so in love with dancing
and then the dance just seemed to drift away...

...and slowly all those nights become a blur,
but oh I loved not knowing who we were.

MIDNIGHT OMELET

Well, I'm cooking up an omelet,
cracking eggs and smacking shells,
chopping onions, lopping peppers,
whipping whisks and casting spells,
shredding cheese and slicing butter,
sloshing wine like cheap cologne.
I'm a Fury. I'm a Beauty,
in my kitchen, all alone.

Now I'm piping in the music,
slapping out the spatula,
rat-a-tatting cross the floor
and singing like a Harpy. Ha!
Got my Indiana Jones hat on-
I'm champing at the bit.
Spark the burners! Sizzle, butter!
Peppers popping! Onions, spit!

Fingers, snap! The music's ripping,
Pinot Grigio's slipping down.
My romance here in the kitchen
is the only show in town.
And this way we never cry.
We live on farce and fire and ice!
Allelujah! Midnight omelet!
It's all spite and paradise.

ALMOST

I don't have grace.
I break an ankle stepping off
the bus. I am a hesitant dancer.
Oh, but this breeze beneath
my bones is quicksilver.

I am not young
but my thoughts burn holes
in the air. In dreams, I take off.
My windows fling out into
the sky. I float on glass.

I am not wise.
I am not brave or beautiful.
But there are nights like this
when, you know, I am
almost.

I'M NOT KEATS

When I have fears that I may cease to be
before my pen has gleaned my teeming brain
of metaphors and rhymes that wantonly
come toppling into stanza and refrain,
how can I sleep? I must get out of bed,
must quick jot down the words I might forget.
There's always too much dancing in my head
and so I must affirm that, as of yet,
the urge to write is what I can't control.
Is there no way to break this blasted curse?
Oh, if I could be Keats and feel my soul
relent and blend into the universe,
that would be nice. But hey, I've always known
I'm just a dog out gnarling on my bone.

NANTUCKET, NOVEMBER

Here on this island, I unclench my fists the moment
I hit the road. Small rocks crunch beneath my
sneakers. Sometimes I lean down to collect an
odd one and let it tumble in my pocket. Mostly I'm
looking at the sky and having my daily dialogue
with God. The wind is turning cold now. It tosses
down my neck in quick quivers. Sprints of light glide
across the fir trees, and atop the glinting pond,
one swan drifts.

I'm in love with all of it.

Too much of my life I've spent knuckling under,
bridling the highs, swallowing the lows, lest the
button-down others catch on to the mess inside.
But here there's no restraint, no boundaries.
Here I'm beckoned in.

Just look at this sky, how it swoops horizon to horizon,
shuffling its moods. This morning it sulked its way
through a smudgy gray. Now it's a cracking blue!
And these roustabout clouds! I've decided they
are painted hour to hour by random angels,
bent on surprise, who can flourish them into
great puffing drums or wisp them into sighs.
Of course there are those days when the angels
tire of hovering and simply sling the clouds across
the sky, proclaiming, "Good enough."

Yes. Good enough. No one here passes sentence.

And when night rolls in, the clouds give way to
stars and beneath the stars, your arms break
free, stretching up, up higher! Turn in circles,
keep turning, let your eyes breathe in all these
stars snapping in the pure black sky. Stare until
you're overcome. Oh, no other place in the world
lays bare so many stars! And this, I believe, is love,
these moments when the soul is utterly overcome.